14351

LATE INTERMEDIATE

SIMPLY *Classics*

Le petit Nègre

Claude Debussy

AF822415

Arranged for Piano Solo by Allan Small

Alfred

A "cakewalk" is an African-American dance that began in the 1800s and became popular in minstrel shows at the turn of the 20th century. It features syncopated, ragtime-like music to which a couple struts arm and arm using high steps. Debussy wrote *Le petit Nègre* in 1909 for another composer's elementary piano method. He closely modeled it after his successful "Golliwog's Cakewalk," the conclusion of his six-movement suite, *Children's Corner*, composed the previous year.

Le petit Nègre

Cakewalk

Claude Debussy (1862–1918)
Arr. Allan Small

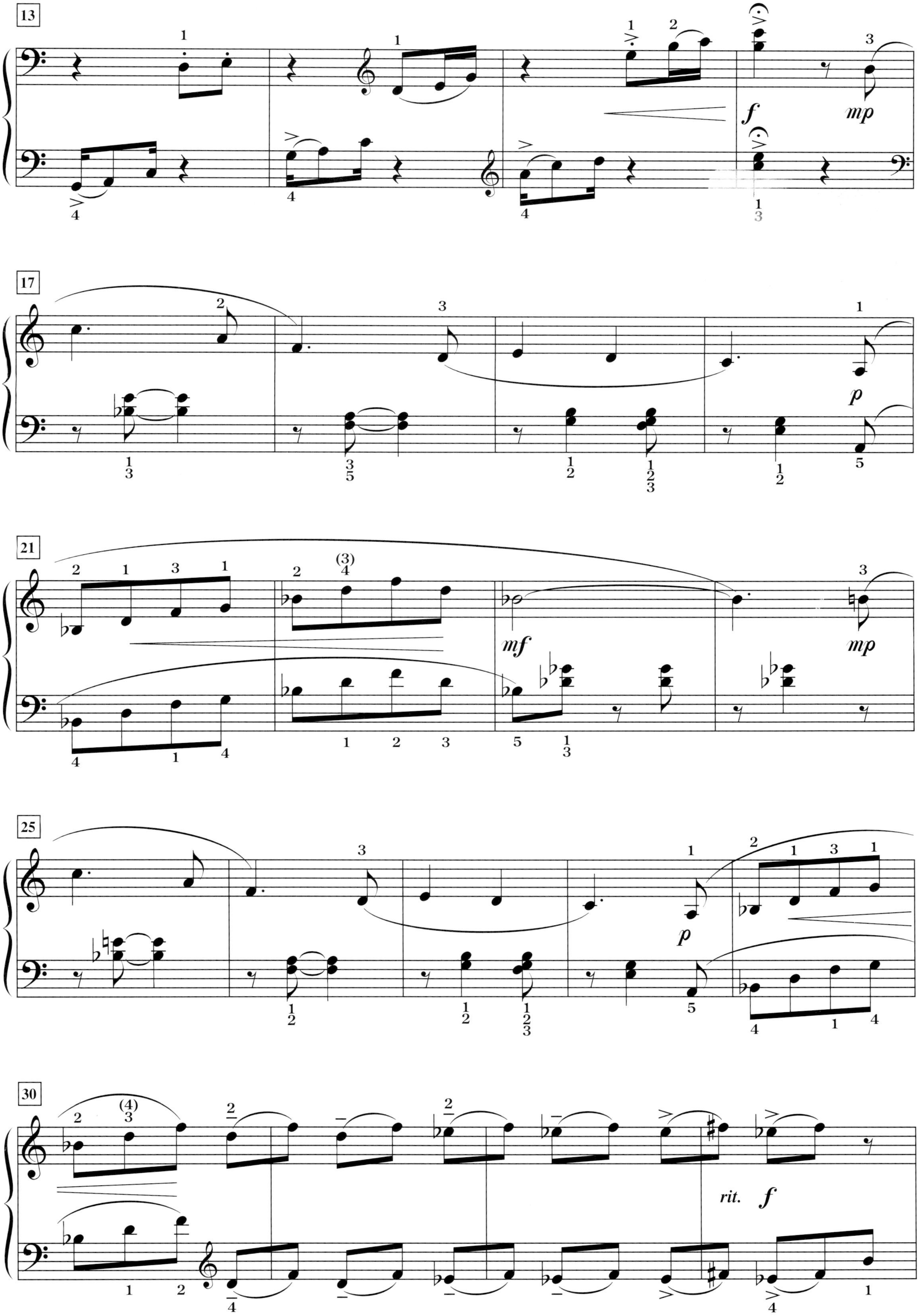
13
f
mp
17
p
21
mf
mp
25
p
30
rit.
f

0 38081 15376 6